LITTLE PRINCESS BOOKS™
Sports for Girls
Coloring & Activity Book

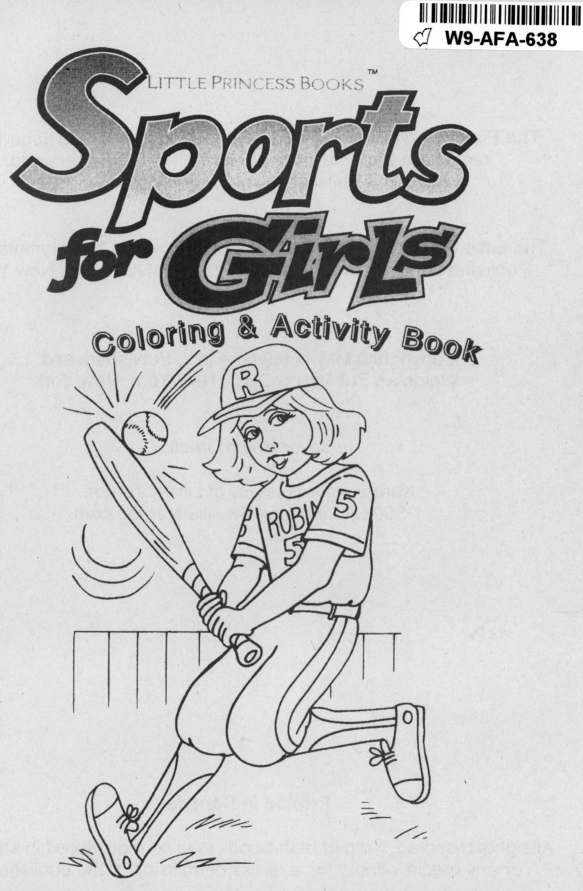

Published by Playmore Inc., Publishers, 58 Main Street, 2nd Floor, Hackensack, N.J. 07601
and Waldman Publishing Corp., 570 Seventh Avenue, New York, N.Y. 10018

Green Grass Practice

Caitlin, Rachel and Maria all play soccer.

The girls warm up by stretching.

In soccer, you have to kick the ball.

Rachel can hit the ball with her head, too.

But only the goalie can touch the ball with her hands.

Rachel kicks the ball into goal to score a point!

Rachel runs fast to kick the ball ahead of her to get it down the field.

The girls are tired by the time they are done with soccer practice.

FOLLOW THE DOTS
to find a star player.

Dreams of Gold

GYMNASTICS

gym

Jessica, Taylor and Alisa became
best friends doing gymnastics together.

Taylor is one of the most flexible girls.

Jessica likes the floor exercises, where
she can do handstands and somersaults.

Jessica and Taylor use a hoop and ball for rhythmic gymnastics.

Alisa works with the rope for her rhythmic gymnastics.

Taylor helps Alisa on the balance beam
to make sure she doesn't fall.

Alisa uses the low beam to learn how to be balanced.

Jessica has to work hard to make her vaults higher.

Alisa learns how to get up on the
uneven parallel bars with a "mount".

Getting off the uneven parallel bars is like flying.

Jessica knows how to land with her feet together
for a perfect dismount.

Someday the girls want to be in the Olympics...
and maybe even win the gold.

SHADOW MATCH
Can you find the shadow to match the picture?

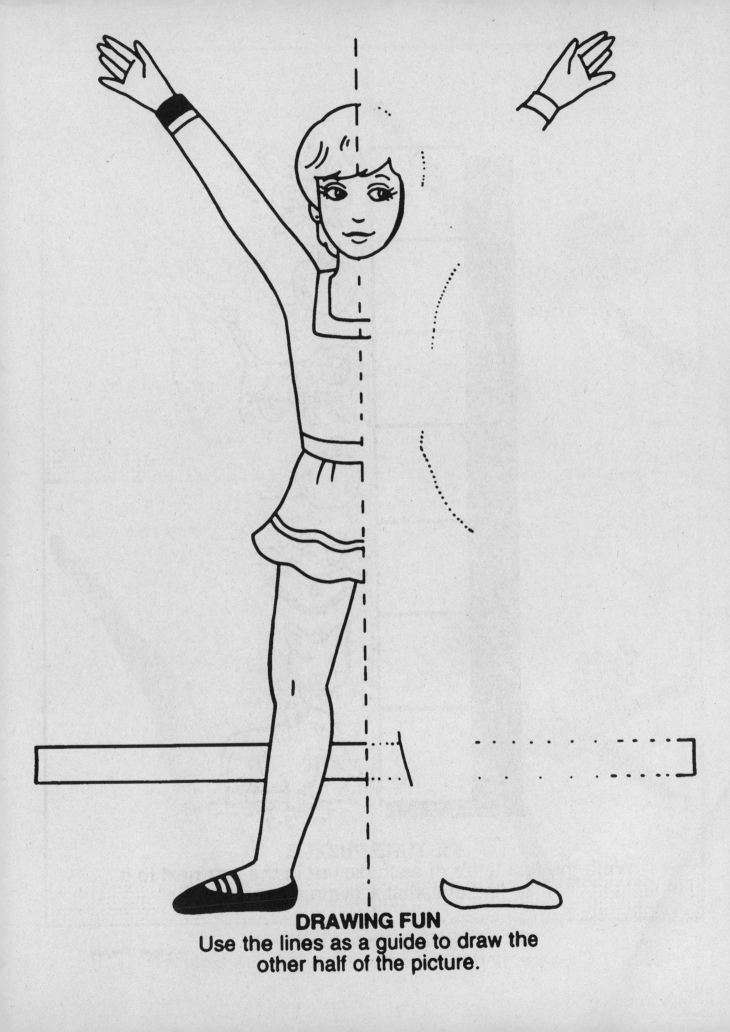

DRAWING FUN
Use the lines as a guide to draw the
other half of the picture.

PICTURE PUZZLE
Write the first letter of each picture in the box next to it,
to find out what a gymnast needs.

Teamwork

Madison and Haley both play softball.

As the pitcher, Haley warms up for her fast ball.

Madison plays first base.

Madison has to know how to catch the ball.

And she has to know how to throw the ball to other team members.

Both girls are good at hitting the ball with the bat.

Sometimes Haley misses the ball. . .
three misses and she strikes out!

Madison swings. . .and hits the ball!

After Madison hits the ball, she runs around the bases.

Madison tags all bases, and slides into home.

Haley is happy that Madison scored a run for their team.

INNING: 9th

SCORE:

ROBINS 10

VISITORS 10

Madison and Haley need to score one more run to win.

On the next pitch, Haley holds her bat still to bunt.

Haley gets a hit, and starts to run to first base.

The other team drops the ball!

Just as the ball is thrown to home plate, Haley slides.

Haley scores the winning run for her team!

Haley and Madison know that it
took teamwork to win the softball game.

FOLLOW THE DOTS
to see who will hit a home run.

Swim Meet

The school swim team is looking for new swimmers.

After school, Katie goes to the pool in her swimsuit.

First thing--everyone gets wet!

"So who can swim the breast stroke?" the swim coach asks.

Katie swims the fastest breast stroke of all the girls.

Now, Katie swims the butterfly stroke,
moving her arms up and down like butterfly wings.

Only six girls make the final list...and Katie is one of them.

"I want to see you all start with a dive off the starting block,"
the coach says.

"Go!" says the coach, and all the girls dive into the pool!

Katie has to swim one lap in each style--
breast stroke, butterfly, and then finish with the backstroke.

Katie has the fastest time...and she makes the team.

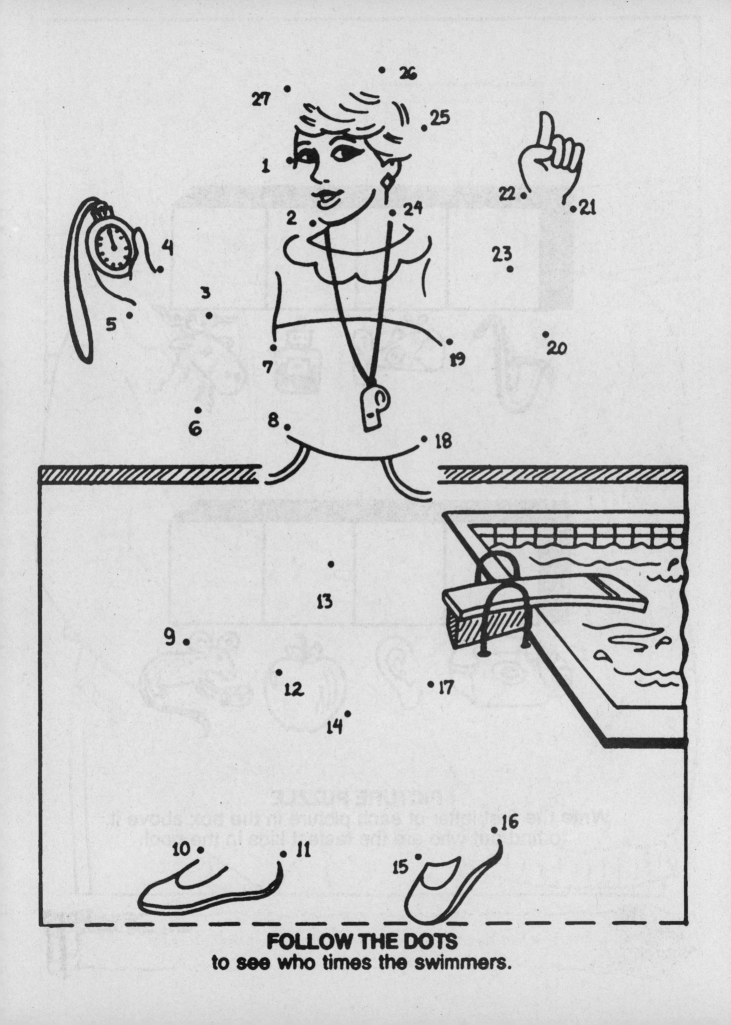

FOLLOW THE DOTS
to see who times the swimmers.

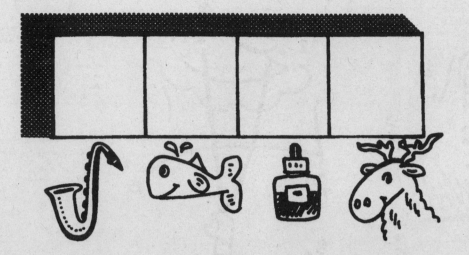

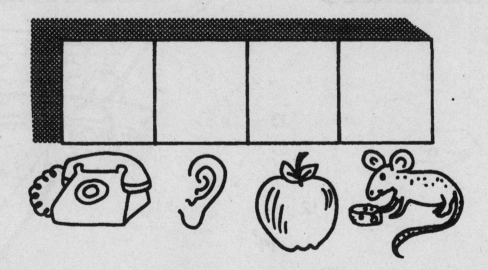

PICTURE PUZZLE
Write the first letter of each picture in the box above it,
to find out who are the fastest kids in the pool.

Blue Ribbon

Ashley's favorite place is the riding stable,
where her pony Casper lives.

Ashley uses brushes to groom Casper.

Casper wears an English saddle and a bridle.

When riding, Ashley wears boots, riding pants and a hard hat to keep her safe in case she falls.

Ashley and Casper love to jump,
and they are taking lessons to get ready for a show.

Heels down and head up, the riding instructor tells Ashley!

Flowers decorate the show arena, and even Casper feels excited.

The jumps in the arena seem really big,
but the biggest fence is a wide jump that is called an oxer!

Ashley and Casper join the other riders in the
warm-up arena to get ready for their class.

Before the jumping class, Ashley and Casper ride in a
non-jumping, "flat" class, that is judged on how well Ashley rides.

Ashley walks Casper into the jumping arena,
and then asks him to canter to the first jump.

Ashley and Casper have to take the jumps in the right order, which is called riding the course.

Ashley and Casper clear the last jump, the big oxer, in perfect form
with Casper's front knees up and Ashley's heels down.

The judge gives Casper and Ashley the blue ribbon for winning the class!

Ashley brings Casper back to his special car.

After the show, Casper grazes and Ashley lazes.

MAZE!
Help Ashley and Casper find their way
through the course to win the show.

PICTURE PUZZLE

Write the first letter of each picture in the box next to it,
to find out what the winner gets.

FOLLOW THE DOTS
to see a graceful girl.

PICTURE PUZZLE
Write the first letter of each picture in the box next to it, to find a winter sport.

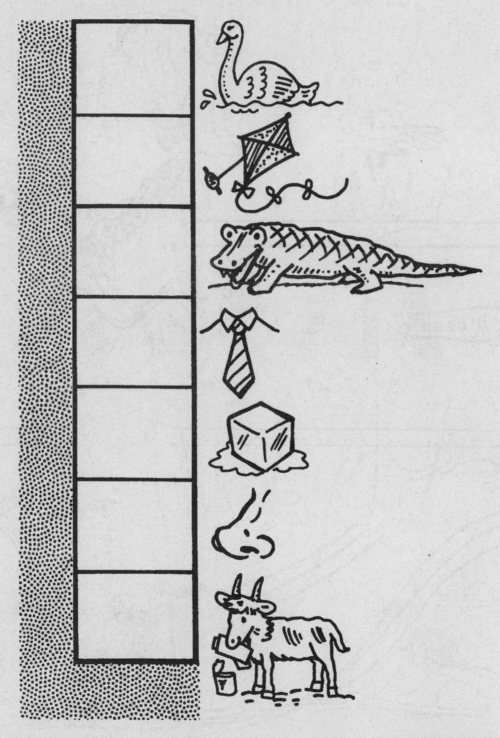

Answer: Skating

The Cheerleaders

As cheerleaders, Laura and Debbie get ready to help their team win.

The cheerleaders wear special uniforms with their school colors.

Debbie and Laura get to lead the cheers at all the football games.

Debbie uses pom-poms for her cheers.

1ST QUARTER
SCORE
MERRYVALE 7
VISITORS 0

Laura cheers when their school scores!

At half-time, the cheerleaders perform with the marching band.

The game is almost over, but their team is behind!

The cheerleaders start their special routine with pom-poms waving.

Debbie does a handstand.

The routine ends with Debbie and Laura
standing on the other girls' shoulders.